LIFE UNDER ICE

MARY M. CERULLO

PHOTOGRAPHY BY
BILL CURTSINGER

TILBURY HOUSE, PUBLISHERS
GARDINER, MAINE

ANTARCTICA

A N T A R C T I C A

Since Antarctica was discovered in 1820, scientists and researchers have braved gale-force winds, mountainous waves, thick fog, and giant icebergs to study one of the few wild places left in our world. Antarctica is a land of extremes—the coldest, driest, windiest, and highest continent. Its name—Antarctica—means the opposite of the Arctic. Ninety percent of the world's ice and 70 percent of the world's fresh water is frozen in antarctic glaciers up to two miles thick. (If they were broken up, there would be enough to supply every person on earth with an ice cube as large as the Great Pyramid!) In the winter, this continent at the bottom of the earth doubles in size as sea ice spreads out from the coast for thousands of miles.

On the surface, Antarctica is a frozen desert. But beneath the sea ice lies a strange oasis, home to an amazing variety of animals and plants that thrive in sub-freezing water, sheltered by the ice that covers their home like a glass roof.

Nature photographer Bill Curtsinger has traveled to this frozen continent many times to dive in its chilly waters and learn about creatures that are able to live in water that is as cold as it can get before you have to walk on it. His dives beneath the ice are adventures in science and survival.

On this trip, Bill and a research team board a helicopter at McMurdo Station, the main center for scientists in Antarctica. The helicopter will drop them off 50 miles away near the edge of the frozen McMurdo Sound. Bill, Paul Dayton from the Scripps Institution of Oceanography, and two other dive partners are planning to study and photograph the animals that live on the bottom of the Southern Ocean—the benthic life.

An emperor penguin watches new arrivals.

2

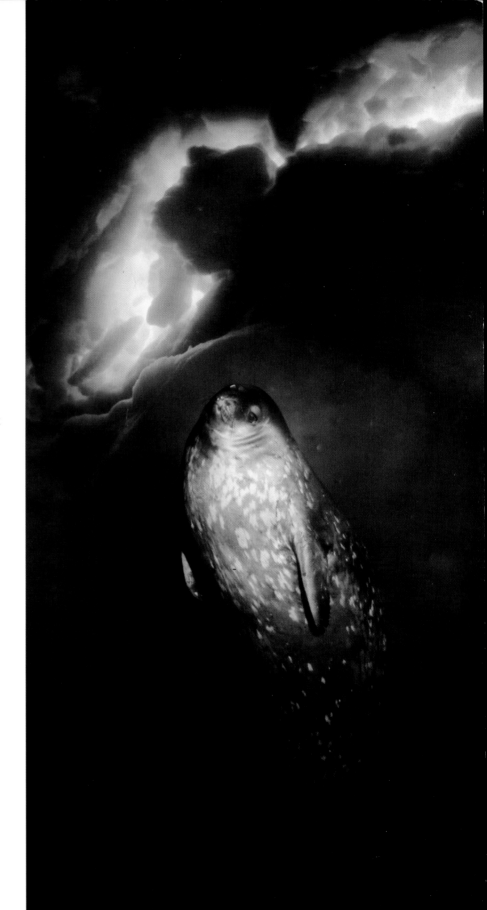

When you dive in Antarctica, you don't just tumble off the side of a boat—or you might end up with a concussion. First you must drill through 5 to 10 feet of sea ice. In the past, underwater explorers used chain saws and dynamite to create diving holes. Today divers use machine-powered augers to drill neat, round tunnels.

Bill and his team land near a breathing hole left by a Weddell seal. The seal had found a crack in the ice, and with its sharp, protruding teeth it chiseled a hole to reach the surface to breathe. This makes the divers' first task easier—all they have to do is enlarge on the Weddell seal's work.

The fur seal (left) and the Weddell seal (right) are two of Antarctica's marine mammals.

To prepare for his dive, Bill wriggles into his dry suit, a well-insulated dive suit that doesn't allow water to get next to his skin like a regular wet suit does. The dry suit covers all of his body except his face and hands. He pulls on insulated gloves that look like giant mittens. Then he slips on his flippers and mask and lifts his dive tank. He gives his dive companions a thumbs-up to show that he is ready to go.

As Bill drops down through the crack in the ice he feels a little like Alice in Wonderland falling down the rabbit's hole. He can't help gasping at the cold water. His lips and cheeks—the only exposed parts of his body—go numb, and within a few seconds his head starts to ache from the cold. Even in summer, water temperatures average 29°F (-1.5°C) to 35.4°F (1.9°C).

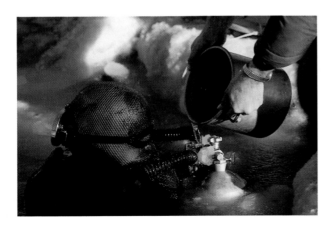

WHY DOESN'T THE OCEAN FREEZE?

The water temperature around Antarctica ranges from 28°F (-1.9°C) to 35.4°F (1.9°C). Fresh water freezes at 32°F (0°C). Salt water freezes at a lower temperature because the dissolved salt blocks the water molecules from linking to form ice crystals. Sea water eventually freezes around 28°F (-1.9°C). (It also melts at a lower temperature, which is why road crews salt icy roads in winter.)

In the ocean, the salt is left in the water during the freezing process. This makes antarctic water saltier than most of the world's oceans.

WINTER OR SUMMER?

When it's winter in the Northern Hemisphere, it is summer in Antarctica. Summer temperatures around the coast average a balmy 32°F (0°C). Winter air temperatures hover around -60°F (-51°C). It's so cold that ice cream stored outside has to be microwaved before it can be eaten!

They are making this dive in October—which is early spring in Antarctica. The water is still as clear as a tropical sea, but by New Year's, when the sun is overhead twenty-four hours a day, billions of tiny floating plants called phytoplankton will be in full bloom. They form a thick sea soup, and Bill would barely be able to see his hand in front of his face. But now, after six months of darkness (May through August), there isn't enough plankton to block Bill's view, and he can clearly see the diving hole from several hundred feet away.

The sun illuminates the open water of the hole like a spotlight. Bill and his dive partners turn back frequently to make sure the hole is still in sight—it's their only link to the world above. Should Bill lose track of the hole, he will retrace his route until his escape hatch is once more in view. Bill shivers—not just from the cold, but as he imagines being trapped beneath a solid ceiling of ice.

Almost immediately a Weddell seal spies Bill. Like an eager puppy, it dashes over to size him up. The curious seal moves in for a closer look until it is nose to nose with Bill's face mask. It circles the divers for a few minutes before swooping past them to poke its head through the dive hole for a quick breath. Then it plunges into deeper water.

The divers also descend, but much more slowly than the seal. Within seconds, the seal returns from the depths to check them out again.

Weddell seals can dive deep and then surface quickly because they don't get the bends like humans do. The bends—also called decompression sickness—are caused by nitrogen gas that becomes trapped in the blood. If a human diver returns to the surface too quickly, the change in pressure may release gas bubbles into the bloodstream that may burst and cause dizziness, paralysis, collapse, and even death. But as a Weddell seal dives, its rib cage partially collapses, squeezing air out of its lungs

until it equalizes the pressure of the water above, keeping the dangerous gas bubbles from forming in its blood. Like whales, these seals store oxygen efficiently, and their blood is pumped away from their flippers to their heart, lungs, and brain where it is needed most.

Scientists have outfitted Weddell seals with instruments that record how deep they dive. They usually dive to 650-1,300 feet (200-400 meters), but can descend to almost 2,000 feet (600 meters) in search of fish, squid, and bottom animals. They can hold their breath for over an hour!

Bill stops a few feet above the ocean floor. It's a beautiful and haunting place, carpeted with sea anemones, sponges, sea stars, brittle stars, sea urchins, sea spiders, worms, and soft corals. It's as colorful as diving on a coral reef in the tropics, and Bill almost forgets how cold he is. As they swim along, Bill and his diving team are careful not to cause damage with their long flippers.

Out of the corner of his eye, Bill sees a chunk of ocean floor drifting slowly upward toward the surface. Unfolding before him is the answer to a mystery that used to puzzle scientists. Every so often someone would find a starfish or a sponge sitting on the surface of the sea ice. Since these bottom-dwellers can't swim, how did they get up there?

Scientists love to find the answer to a mystery! By careful observation they discovered that every spring, fresh water from melting ice pours off the land and the surface ice and sinks to the bottom of the ocean. Slightly colder than the surrounding salty water, this "anchor ice" freezes as soon as it touches a rock, mud, or an unlucky animal lying on the ocean bottom.

As the bits of anchor ice gradually merge, it becomes more buoyant and floats up, carrying sea stars, sponges, and an occasional slow-moving fish up through the water until they bump into the surface ice and freeze onto the underside of the ice. Gradually the ice above melts away, exposing the sea stars and other creatures that would normally be living on the ocean floor.

Far left: A diver watches as anchor ice floats toward the surface. Top: Colorful sea anemones cover the ocean floor.

Bill's diving team follows a slope down to a depth
of about 120 feet (37 meters)—it's like taking a
slow elevator down a twelve-story building. Paul
is a benthic ecologist who is diving today to learn
more about sponge growth in antarctic waters.
He finds a giant sponge larger than himself,
and while he measures it, Bill swims around him
capturing shots of his work. Paul is careful not to
push too hard on the sponge for fear of damaging
its delicate structure.

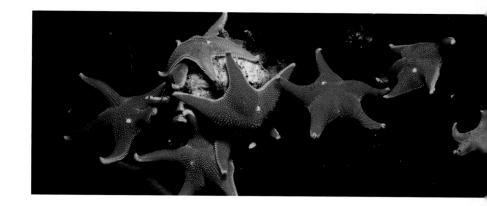

After about a half hour, Bill's hands and feet have
grown numb. His fingers are so stiff he can no
longer adjust the focus on his camera, so he signals
his partners that it's time to go up. They rise up
to a depth of 30 feet (9 meters), where they stop
and allow their bodies to decompress for several
minutes. Returning to their dive hole in the ice
takes longer than they expect because distances
in crystal-clear water seem much closer than they
really are.

Diving in cold water uses much more energy than diving in warmer seas, and the divers rise to the surface completely exhausted. Bill and the others crawl into a tent and crank up a kerosene stove to get warm. They are going to spend three nights in the tent so they can make several more dives before returning to the science station. Each member of the team devours a stack of steaks, then settles into his or her thick, down sleeping bag.

Before turning off his headlamp, Bill writes down his thoughts and makes some quick sketches of the strange animals he has seen. He has a lot of questions to ask the scientists back at the science station and is looking forward to hearing their explanations and ideas.

Bill falls asleep soon, but he tosses and turns all night, and never really warms up. His dreams are jumbled with images of ice and snow. He wakes up before 6 A.M. The sun is still as bright as it was when they went to bed, but it's freezing cold in the tent. The condensation from their breath has formed a coating of rime ice inside the tent. Their toothpaste is frozen solid. The bravest one climbs out of his sleeping bag to start the stove. Soon the temperature inside the tent is bearable and coffee is made. Getting ready for another dive, Bill reminds himself that the water under the ice will be warmer than the air above.

Bill and the dive team spend four days out on the
sea ice before the helicopter comes to take them
back to McMurdo Station. After a long, hot shower
and a huge meal at headquarters, Bill pulls out his
journal and peppers the scientists sitting around
the table with his questions. A geologist, a marine
biologist, a meteorologist, a physical oceanographer,
an astronomer, and even a veterinarian are all
working on various projects at the science station.

Bill has dived in all the seas of the world, but diving
in Antarctica still amazes him. Nowhere else do
marine animals face the challenges they have to
contend with under the ice. Here, they have to
swim in water cold enough to freeze their blood.
It is dark for six months of the year, and without
sunlight to fuel plankton growth, plant-eaters have
no food. Bottom animals risk becoming trapped
in anchor ice. Air-breathing seals have to find holes
just to breath. Penguins sometimes commute hun-
dreds of miles between their nesting sites and the
sea to find food for their chicks.

Krill are shrimp-like animals eaten by most of the other animals in Antarctica's marine foodweb.

Bill asks the scientists around the table, "Why do the animals put up with the cold and ice?" The researchers, digging into a plate of freshly baked cookies, respond in a chorus, "FOOD!"

The Southern Ocean is like a giant food factory, they explain to Bill between bites. Strong currents act like a spoon in a pot, stirring up a thick soup of nutrients. Minerals from melting glaciers mix with decaying plants and animals from the ocean floor, and when you add abundant sunlight, you have ideal conditions for an underwater greenhouse. Tiny plants called ice algae grow in pockets on the underside of sea ice, and phytoplankton—microscopic floating plants—bloom in the water near the surface. These are eaten by shrimp-like creatures called krill. Each krill is only the size of a human thumb, but when there are thousands of them together, they can turn the ocean pink.

There isn't much variety to eat in Antarctica—the food web is simple—so krill are very important. Penguins, squid, fish, seals, seabirds, and even enormous whales all eat a steady diet of krill.

Bill has spotted several kinds of whales swimming in the open water surrounding the antarctic continent. Well insulated from the cold by thick layers of blubber, killer whales, minkes, humpbacks, finbacks, and even the giant blue whales feast on the krill. In fact, the word "krill" is the Norwegian term for "whale food."

Top left: Giants of the Antarctica include a giant isopod and (bottom) a giant sea spider.

Bill doodles a picture of a krill on his napkin, which prompts him to recall the sketch he made in his notebook of an animal on the ocean floor that he couldn't identify. He turns to Paul Dayton sitting at the far end of the table and asks, "What was that huge, prehistoric-looking 'bug'? It seemed familiar, but I've never seen one so big—it looked like something you'd see in an Age of Dinosaurs diorama in a natural history museum."

Paul laughs and replies that what Bill saw was a giant isopod, an animal related to a shrimp. Bill is amazed. He's seen thousands of isopods wriggling around in rocky tidepools, but each was only the size of a fingernail. "This isopod had to be five inches long!"

Paul explains that it's a phenomenon called "gigantism" found in extremely cold seas. Here in Antarctica you can find sea spiders as large as dinner plates, jellyfish the size of umbrellas, sponges big enough to stand inside, and sea stars almost two feet across!

"Maybe it's because the animals have found a habitat that no one else wanted, so there's no competition for food or space," suggests another scientist. "With less pressure from competitors and predators, they don't have to rush growing up so they grow large, if slowly." Paul explains that the cold water slows their body functions and leads to a longer lifespan. One starfish was known to have lived thirty-nine years!

"Cold-blooded animals also move slower in frigid water," points out Allan Child, a scientist from the Smithsonian Institution who is studying sea spiders. Even ice fish and giant isopods move so slowly they have been caught in anchor ice. Bill remembers watching sea spiders (called pycnogonids) creep slowly across the ocean floor on their spindly legs. "They're the original slow-motion animals," agrees Allan. "You just want to get behind them and push!"

A member of the dive team eyes a sea sponge big enough to sleep inside.

One scientist who really knows what it takes to survive in Antarctica is Gerald Kooyman from the Scripps Institution of Oceanography. He spends ten weeks every other year camping on the ice near McMurdo Station to study the deep-diving ability of seals and emperor penguins. It's a big change from the beaches near his home in Southern California.

Gerald and his research group have made many interesting discoveries. Unlike other penguins, emperor penguins are the only penguins to winter over on the antarctic ice. They were thought to stay close to their home colonies all year long. But by attaching electronic backpacks to the penguins' feathers, the researchers found that the birds swim all around the Ross Sea, an area the size of France. They can stay underwater at least 22 minutes and can dive deeper than 1,500 feet (460 meters).

Penguins are designed for life in the sea and on the ice—which is fortunate since these birds can't fly. A streamlined body, paddle-like feet, and a layer of blubber beneath watertight feathers make penguins speedy and comfortable underwater. As penguins preen their feathers, they spread oil from a gland near their tail that waterproofs them.

Feathers also help to regulate their body temperature on land. When penguins feel cold they turn their black backs toward the sun to absorb its warmth. They face the sun with their white chests when they want to cool down. Bill remembers photographing a group of Adélie penguins sunning themselves on a chunk of sea ice, their white bibs turned toward the sun. Suddenly a leopard seal leaped onto the ice behind them and, startled, the flock turned as one to face the predator. The seal managed to grab a penguin near the edge of the ice. It dove back into the water with its prey. This triggered a panic among the remaining penguins but none of them dared to jump off the ice into the water.

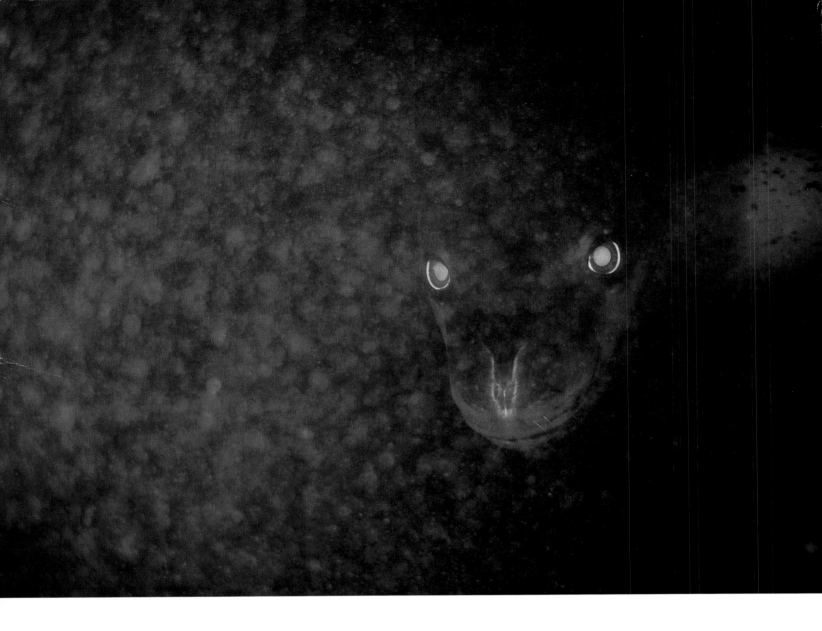

The leopard seal emerged from the shadows at 120 feet below the surface.

Bill himself recalls a close encounter with a leopard seal. It happened on a day when Bill's camera wasn't working right. The flash attachment, called a strobe light, was misfiring, flashing on and off continuously. Bill was diving 120 feet below the surface and there wasn't anything he could do to fix it, so he kept the strobe behind him where it wouldn't blind the scientist trying to do his work. Suddenly Bill felt a tug on his strobe light. He turned around to come face to face with a big leopard seal! Bill yanked the strobe away from the curious animal and thinking quickly, flashed a photo!

Then a flock of emperor penguins zoomed by. Each bird left a trail of bubbles as the water pressure squeezed out the air trapped between their feathers. The leopard seal took off in pursuit. This predator spends the winter feeding on krill, but in the spring, when the penguins are hunting for food for their chicks, the leopard seal feasts on the fatty birds.

The ice fish has antifreeze in its veins.

Although there are more than 20,000 species of fish in the world, only 120 kinds can live in cold antarctic waters. Bill knows that most fish are cold-blooded and take on the temperature of the surrounding water. So how do these fish keep from freezing in sub-freezing water? He learns that one fish in particular is well suited for life in antarctic waters.

The antarctic ice fish has a natural antifreeze that runs through its veins instead of red blood. (Red blood cells don't carry oxygen well in low temperatures.) It also has a large heart and wide blood vessels to help pump its thin, clear blood through its body. Its colorless blood gives the ice fish a pale, ghostly appearance. Bill has heard that antarctic whalers used to call it the white crocodile fish because of its large mouth with many long teeth.

Antarctica's ice is important to creatures living below it and on top of it. Like a lid covering the ocean, it keeps heat in so the water is always warmer than the air. The underside of the ice supports a marine meadow of microscopic plants that feed krill and the rest of the antarctic food web. The top side provides a relatively safe refuge for penguins from leopard seals—a place where the birds can rest, nest, and raise their young. When there are changes in the sea ice—either from natural cycles or brought on by human activities—the effects are felt in Antarctica and far away.

We now know that the penguin population and the krill population rise and fall depending on the amount of ice surrounding Antarctica in the winter. For nearly thirty years, Susan and Wayne Trivelpiece have been studying Adélie penguins on King George Island near the tip of the Antarctic Peninsula. Susan explains, "If the sea ice is heavy and extends over large areas where the krill spawn, then most of the newly hatched krill will survive and there will be enough food for the young penguins."

But winter temperatures on the peninsula have risen about 4° to 5°F (15°C) over the last fifty years, changing the sea ice distribution. The Trivelpieces have recorded a 50 percent decline in Adélie penguins returning to their study site, and they think that the young penguins are not getting enough food because there are fewer krill.

Other penguin colonies are threatened by too much ice. On the opposite side of Antarctica, several huge icebergs have broken away from the Ross Ice Shelf and piled up in the Ross Sea. Now, instead of swimming from their feeding grounds to their nesting grounds, thousands of adult Adélie penguins have to walk across the ice, a trip that can take five times as long. Scientists believe that many won't survive the long march.

Changes in Antarctica also affect other parts of the world because this continent of ice is like a global air conditioner. Winds and currents flowing away from Antarctica circulate cool temperatures around the earth. Heavy, salty water, called Antarctic Bottom Water can be traced all the way to the North Pole. Slightly warmer, fresher water from the melting of the ice sheet, called Antarctic Intermediate Water, can be found as far north as New York City!

Even in faraway Antarctica, scientists may be seeing evidence of global warming. Temperature differences of just a few degrees can start changes. Ice sheets are breaking apart. The Ross Sea, the saltiest sea in the Southern Ocean, is becoming less salty because of reduced sea ice and melting of the West Antarctic Ice Sheet.

There are other changes, too. In 1985 scientists discovered that there was a hole in the thin ozone layer of the atmosphere 7 to 15 miles above Antarctica. The ozone layer protects the earth from harmful ultraviolet (UV) radiation from the sun. After three years of monitoring, they found the culprit: a group of chemicals called CFCs found in refrigerators, solvents, and spray cans could destroy ozone even as far away as above Antarctica. Higher UV radiation has been linked to increases in skin cancer in humans and may cause changes to the phytoplankton and krill, which affects all the animals within the antarctic food web.

But in spite of these changes, Antarctica has the distinction of still being the most peaceful, untouched place on earth. No wars have ever been fought there, no country owns it, and tourists and scientists don't need to have a passport or anyone's permission to visit. This Zone of Peace offers researchers from different fields and different countries something very rare: the chance to cooperate and learn more about this continent and the world beyond. Because it is cleaner than anywhere else on earth, Antarctica is an ideal outdoor laboratory for studying weather, the stars, climate change, and human impacts on the environment. Its desolate surface even serves as a training area for Mars exploration.

Seals huddle together on the antarctic ice.

As the last natural wilderness, Antarctica still lures those seeking adventure. Too much so, worries Bill Curtsinger, who has seen the impact of more tourists and even scientists on the continent. "About 15,000 tourists and 4,000 scientists visit Antarctica each year. By 2010 it's projected that 1.5 million people a season will come to Antarctica. How can we make sure they don't destroy the very qualities they are coming to experience?"

A new kind of research is now taking place in Antarctica, called the Human Impacts Research Program. These scientists, mostly from Australia, study the impact of visitors and vehicles such as helicopters, snowmobiles, and Zodiacs invading the breeding sites of seals, petrels, and penguins. They are also examining ways to clean up abandoned worksites without causing more damage. Until the mid-1980s the preferred way of disposing of garbage was to push it out onto the sea ice. When the ice broke up in spring, the debris would go away. All of us now know that there is no "away."

Their work is leading to new rules of conduct for tourists and scientists to make sure that wildlife and this unique frozen wilderness are disturbed as little as possible.

Even those of us who will never visit Antarctica can appreciate the value in keeping it as natural and unspoiled as possible. The countries of the world have agreed that Antarctica will remain free—from oil drilling, exploitation, and war. It's important to preserve wild places where our imaginations can roam free.

LET'S FIND OUT MORE

There are many ways to find out about Antarctica without actually going there—through books and the Internet.

WEBSITES

- **Antarctica: The Farthest Place Close to Home:**
www.amnh.org/education/resources/antarctica/index.php
This rich curriculum resource has been put together by the American Museum of Natural History. Each curriculum material includes a timeline, teacher strategies for implementing activities and readings in the classroom, suggestions for final projects in which students apply their new skills and knowledge, and National Science and Social Studies Standards correlation. Topics include: Continent of Extremes; Day and Night Cycles; Extreme Temperatures; Extreme Winds; Maps; Exploration; Navigation and GPS; Organisms; and Hazards to Humans.
- **Classroom Antarctica:**
http://classroomantarctica.aad.gov.au/
- **Gulf of Maine Aquarium:** www.gma.org
- **Space Available, Antarctica Live from Antarctica2:**
http://quest.arc.nasa.gov/antarctica2/index.html
- **Antarctic Facts:** www.coolantarctica.com
- **Teachers Experiencing Antarctica and the Artic:**
http://tea.rice.edu
TEA is a program sponsored by the National Science Foundation (NSF) in which teachers are selected to travel to the Antarctic and the Arctic for a field season to participate in ongoing research. TEA is a partnership between teachers, researchers, students, school districts, and communities. The website includes online journals from teachers in the field, classroom activities and links to websites on education, polar research, and exploration.

READ ABOUT IT

Cerullo, Mary. **Ocean Detectives: Solving the Mysteries of the Sea**. Austin, TX: Raintree Steck-Vaughn, 2000.
Chester, Jonathan. **A for Antarctica**. Berkeley, CA: Tricycle Press, 1998.
Dewey, Jennifer Owings. **Antarctic Journal: Four Months at the Bottom of the World**. New York: HarperCollins, 2001.
McMillan, Bruce. **Summer Ice: Life Along the Antarctic Peninsula**. Boston: Houghton Mifflin, 1995.
Potter, Keith R. **Seven Weeks on an Iceberg**. San Francisco: Chronicle Books, 1999.

GLOSSARY

anchor ice This ice forms as colder, fresh water sinks to the ocean floor and freezes on whatever it touches, including rocks, mud, or bottom animals. pp 10, 11
auger A tool with a spiral cutting edge to bore holes in wood, ice, earth, etc. p 3
bends (decompression sickness) A condition that may occur in a diver when gas in the bloodstream from breathing compressed air is released too quickly, like removing the cap from a bottle of carbonated water. p 8
benthic Bottom-dwelling. pp 2, 10
CFCs (chlorofluorocarbons) A group of chemicals found in refrigerators, solvents, and spray cans which can destroy ozone. p 33
continental ice sheet An ice sheet formed from snow accumulating, year after year, until it compresses into ice. This forms glaciers, which can move slowly down mountain valleys. Antarctic ice sheets are 12,000 feet (3,658 meters) thick in places. pp 1, 33

ecologist A scientist who studies the relationships among plants, animals, and their environment. p 13

fast ice Ice that is attached to the land. It never melts. There is water beneath it.

food web A complex interrelationship of who eats whom. pp 19, 33

gigantism A condition found around the poles in which normally small marine creatures grow to unusually large size. pp 20, 21

global warming The theory that carbon dioxide and other gases produced by the burning of fossil fuels are trapped in the upper atmosphere, absorbing and reflecting heat back to earth. p 33

iceberg A mass of ice broken off from a glacier and floating in the sea. p 31

isopod A small crustacean that resembles a shrimp with a flat, oval body. p 20

krill Small, shrimp-like creatures that exist in huge numbers in antarctic waters (and elsewhere). They are important food for many other animals. pp 18-19, 27, 33

ozone hole A hole in a thin ozone layer that protects the earth from harmful ultraviolet (UV) radiation from the sun. p 33

pack ice Broken pieces of sea ice that have pushed together into one big mass of ice. This is where seals give birth to their pups.

peninsula Land surrounded on three sides by water.

phytoplankton Microscopic plants that drift with the ocean currents. pp 7, 19, 33

predator An animal that eats other animals. p 23

rime ice A coating of tiny ice crystals that forms on grass, leaves, etc. from moisture in the air. p 15

sea ice Formed by the freezing of sea water. Sea ice floats on the surface of the water. Under the stress of wind and ocean currents, sea ice cracks and moves. Sea ice is also called annual ice, because it breaks up in summer. As the temperature warms, it becomes too dangerous to try to drive vehicles on it. pp 1, 10, 23, 28, 31, 33, 35

shelf ice Continental ice that flows out from the land to the sea surface and floats on the ocean. It can be 1,640 feet (500 meters) thick in places. pp 1, 33

solvent A liquid that dissolves another substance; a powerful cleaning solution. p 33

ultraviolet radiation (UV) Light rays that produce harmful effects on humans, animals, and phytoplankton. p 33

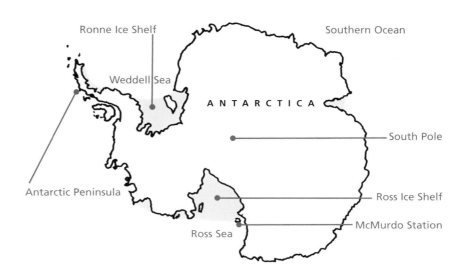

TILBURY HOUSE, PUBLISHERS

2 Mechanic Street, Gardiner, Maine 04345

800–582–1899 • www.tilburyhouse.com

Our thanks to: Karen Baker, Ph.D., Long-Term Ecological Research Program/Information Management, for reviewing the manuscript; Baldo Marinovic, Institute of Marine Sciences, University of California, Santa Cruz; Paul Dayton, Ph.D., Scripps Institute of Oceanography; Charles Galt, Biological Sciences, University of California Long Beach; Myles Gordon, Ed.D., Director of Education, American Museum of Natural History, for curriculum guidance; Terry Klinger, Ph.D., University of Washington School of Marine Affairs; National Geographic Image Sales for the use of Bill Curtsinger's photo of the leopard seal at the top of page 26; the staff and advisory board of the National Science Foundation and its Teachers Experiencing the Arctic and Antarctica Program (TEA) for inspiration; and Gordon Robilliard, Entrix Biological Consultants.

Library of Congress Cataloging-in-Publication Data

Cerullo, Mary M.

Life under ice / Mary M. Cerullo ; photography by Bill Curtsinger.

p. cm.

Summary: Follows marine photographer Bill Curtsinger as he dives under the ice at Antarctica to learn about the plants and animals that thrive in this extreme habitat.

ISBN 0-88448-246-4 (hardcover : alk. paper)

1. Marine organisms—Antarctica—Juvenile literature.   [1. Marine animals—Antarctica.
2. Marine plants—Antarctica. 3. Antarctica.]   I. Curtsinger, Bill, 1946-   , ill. II. Title.

QH84.2.C47 2003

578.777—dc21

2002154451

Designed by Geraldine Millham, Westport, MA

Editorial and production work by Jennifer Bunting, Audrey Maynard, and Barbara Diamond.

Color scans by Integrated Composition Systems, Spokane, WA

Printing and binding by Worzalla Publishing, Stevens Point, WI